published in the united states by Rocky Heights Print & Binding

visit us at www.readkaleidoscope.com

kaleidoscope, *kids bibles reimagined*

library of congress cataloging-in-publication data is available upon request
ISBN - 978-1-64911-007-7

cover art by becca godfrey (www.beccagodfrey.com)

for neal, leslie, gabbie, grace, and maggie
for living in light of the gospel
for being the first to really believe the vision
...and for all the early morning runs.

WELCOME TO KALEIDOSCOPE

First of all, thank you for picking up a copy of Kaleidoscope! We are glad to have you. In the following pages, you'll experience the Bible in a whole new way.

Kaleidoscope emerged from the need to retell the Bible for elementary-aged children at a level between a "little kid" Bible and an adult translation. In a way, we are a happy medium.

At Kaleidoscope, we are producing single volumes for every book of the Bible. We design them to read like chapter books, so you'll turn pages and look forward with anticipation to the next volume.

But don't let the fact that we are focused on kids deter you if you are a "big kid!" Good children's books are almost always as good for adults as they are for kids.

Get excited! In the pages that follow, you'll see God's fantastic good news. Our prayer is that his kindness, gentleness, and love will melt our hearts and make us more like Jesus.

I grinned with delight through each chapter of *Living Water*! If *The Jesus Storybook Bible* had an older sibling—this would be it. If you have a young reader who has outgrown the Bible-based options on his or her bookshelf, make space for this ASAP!

-Caroline Saunders
Bible teacher and author of LifeWay girls' study *Better Than Life: How to Study the Bible and Like It*

Kaleidoscope's aim is big — to help kids see how all the stories in the Bible comprise one grand, beautiful story of redemption. As a parent, Bible teacher, and church planter, I can't commend this approach to Bible study enough.

-Amy Gannett
Tiny Theologians

Living Water is accessible, engaging, and inviting, and children who read this adaptation will undoubtedly find the book of John to be more accessible, engaging, and inviting as well when they open an adult translation. I am deeply grateful to have this resource to help guide my children into discovering and loving the Bible for themselves.

-Abbey Wedgeworth
author of *Held: 31 Biblical Reflections on God's Comfort and Care in the Sorrow of Miscarriage* and curator of the annual *Gentle Leading Advent Devotional for Moms*

As a mom, I longed for a kid's Bible that would keep our children engaged while offering a faithful account of the stories in Scripture. Kaleidoscope is entertaining, responsible, and gospel driven!

-Hunter Beless
Executive Director of Journeywomen

You hold in your hand a tool that will unleash the unhindered gospel on the hearts of your kids, and there really is nothing more important than that.

-Dick Cain
Rainbow City Presbyterian

In over 20 years of Children's Ministry, this is one of the most inspiring tools I have seen to help kids (and their parents) experience the Bible in a creative and powerful way!

-Jason Houser
Seeds Family Worship

My son loves reading Kaleidoscope because he learns new details about old Bible stories and some new stories he has never heard before. As a mom, I love how Kaleidoscope carefully explains tricky passages while connecting each story to the bigger story of the Bible.

-Maggie Combs
author of *Motherhood Without All the Rules* and *Unsupermommy*

Thoughtfully crafted and such an exciting resource for any child!

-Korrie Johnson
@goodbookmom

CREATORS

Chris Ammen is the founder of Kaleidoscope and a Children's Pastor in Tuscaloosa, AL. He has a BA and M.Ed. in Elementary Education as well as an M.Div. from Covenant Seminary. When not writing, Chris loves spending time with his wife, Sarah, and their four awesome kiddos!

Maggie is a graduate of Creative Circus in Atlanta where she studied graphic design. When not illustrating, she enjoys her cats, reading, baking, and all things cozy. You can see more of Maggie's work at www.maggiesnead.com.

TABLE OF CONTENTS

INTRODUCTION

How do we know what we know about Jesus? That's a great question! Part of God's plan all along was to send his son from heaven to earth. Jesus was fully man and fully God. A big part of this plan was that Jesus would not live alone. He befriended twelve people, called disciples.

The disciples learned from Jesus, followed him, and helped him as he cared for thousands of people during his lifetime. With the Holy Spirit's leading, some of the disciples spent the rest of their lives writing about Jesus and what it means to live as a Christian.

John was one of those men. So were Simon Peter, Matthew, and others. So, how do we know what we know about Jesus? Through men like John, who walked with, talked to, and learned from Jesus - and then wrote about him.

John's writing is a type of book we call a "gospel." There are three other gospels: Matthew, Mark, and Luke. John's gospel is unique in a few ways:
- There is no birth story. You won't find the book of John taught much around Christmas!
- John wrote to both Jews and Gentiles.
- John wants his readers to know that Jesus is the Son of God, the long-awaited Messiah.

- John uses lots of word pictures to describe Jesus. He is the light of the world, good shepherd, bread of life, door for the sheep, vine, and living water.
- John tells us about lots of cool miracles and healings Jesus did to show us that he is, in fact, God's Son.

John uses all of these features to weave together a beautiful picture of Jesus's life. Jesus came to tell people about his Father. He also warned the world of the danger of sin. Sin is anything we do that is not what God wants for our life. It is living only for ourselves when the Bible says we should live to worship God and love others. The Bible tells us our sin deserves death, but that God sent Jesus to die for us so that whoever believes in him would not perish, but have eternal life.

Because of this, and more, John is one of the most well-loved books in all the Bible. When you read the book of John, you will experience a range of feelings and emotions. We will celebrate together when Jesus feeds thousands of people. We will feel sad when Jesus and his mom share a special moment right before his death. We might even feel angry when people do not listen to Jesus.

Whatever the case, we are excited to be on this journey with you. Let's dive in together and learn more about Jesus!

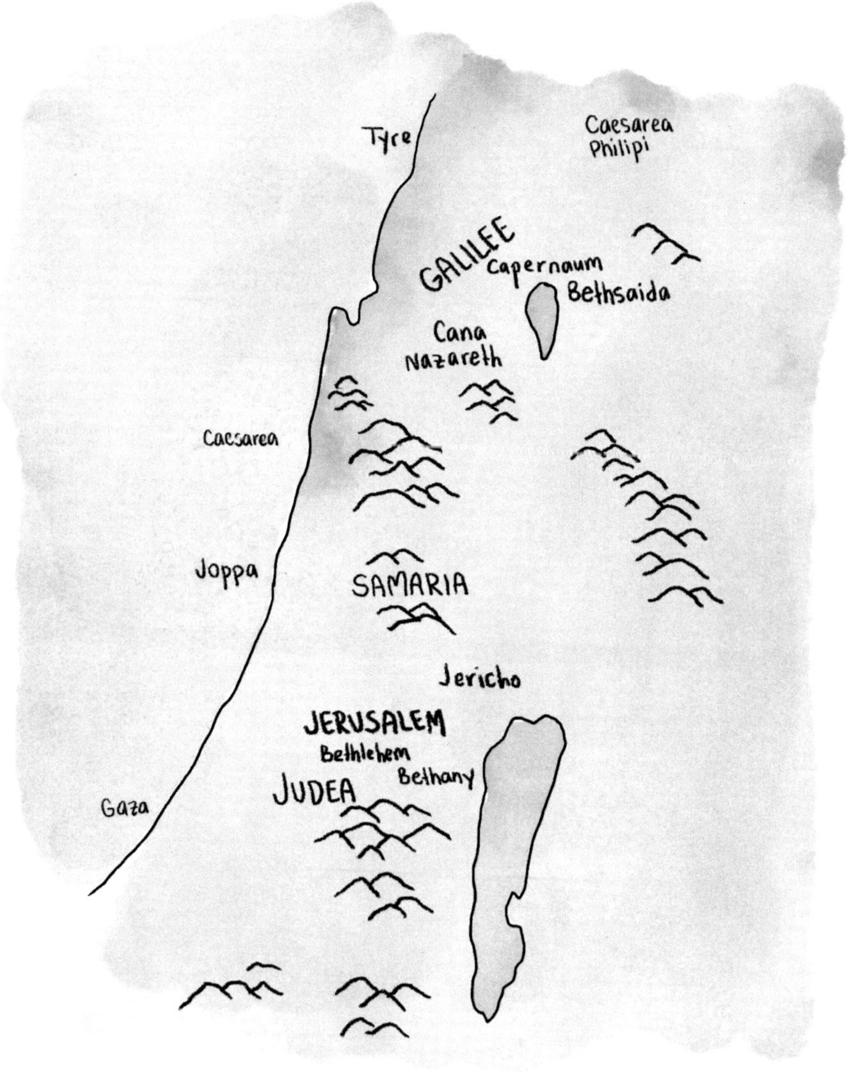
Tyre
Caesarea
Philipi
GALILEE
Capernaum
Bethsaida
Cana
Nazareth
Caesarea
Joppa
SAMARIA
Jericho
JERUSALEM
Bethlehem
Bethany
JUDEA
Gaza

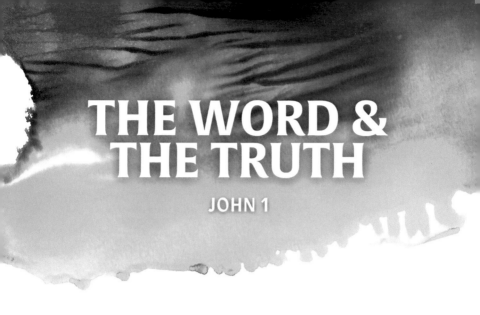

THE WORD & THE TRUTH

JOHN 1

How do you begin to describe a man who changed the entire course of history?

What if he lived before history even began?

What if we could know him?

His name is Jesus. He is the very Son of God. He was with God in the beginning. He made all things. He tells us what is true and beautiful about God. His life is the very light of humankind, showing us how to live in a dark world.

God sent a man named John to tell the world about Jesus. John explained, "Jesus will bring light to the world, but his brothers and sisters will choose to stay in the darkness. However, all who do see him for who he truly is will become children of God."

Children of God!? Did you hear that? Not only can you know about God's Son, but you can become as close as a son or daughter!

1

But Jesus was not a high and mighty king who lived in some unreachable space. No, Jesus came and lived with people like you and me! Jesus was the very presence of God, yet he was also a human. He came to live with us so we would see God in all his beauty and glory.

One day, John was teaching about Jesus when some people known as priests approached him. Priests were the spiritual leaders of the Jews. They taught people about God, but they hadn't come to understand that Jesus was God's Son.

Doubting John's authority, the priests questioned, "Who do you think you are? Are you Elijah the prophet?"

John answered, "I am not Elijah, and I am not the Christ (another name for the Savior they had been waiting for). I am just a man, a voice crying out, telling people to make their hearts ready for the Savior to come."

These priests, however, had other motives. Their questions were not nearly as innocent as they seemed. You see, the Pharisees had sent the priests to question John. Pharisees were a group of Jews who thought they were big and important. Pharisees thought God would love them if they just kept all the rules. But of course, that is silly. Because of sin, we will never be able to follow all the rules. The whole Bible tells us that we need a rescuer, but the Pharisees were offended by the idea that they couldn't save themselves!

So the priests continued to press John for an answer. "If you are not the Christ or Elijah, why are you baptizing people?"

John answered, "I baptize with water, but among you is standing someone so great that I am not even worthy to untie his sandals!" John knew that Jesus was more than a man and worthy of great honor.

The very next day, John saw Jesus coming from far off. John recognized him immediately and called out, "Everyone look! The Lamb of God, who takes away the sins of the world! He is who I told you would come! I baptize with water, but this man baptizes with the Holy Spirit. I even saw the Spirit rest over him. That is is how I know that he is indeed the Son of God!"

The next day, as John was with two of his disciples, Jesus walked by again. John said one more time, "Look, the Lamb of God!" The two disciples immediately began to follow behind Jesus.

Suddenly, Jesus turned to the men and asked, "Who are you looking for?"

The disciples replied, "Rabbi (which means teacher), where are you staying?"

3

Jesus answered, "Come with me."

The two disciples stayed with Jesus that night. The next day one of the two disciples, named Andrew, hurried to tell his brother, Simon, that he had found the Messiah (another word for Christ). The one they had waited for was finally here! Together, they rushed back to begin the adventure of a lifetime by following Jesus!

When Jesus first met Simon, he said, "Your name will now be Cephas (which means Peter)." Renaming someone may seem a bit strange to us today. But in Jesus's time, this was a source of pride! Simon's new name meant "rock." Perhaps God was making Peter strong!

The next day, Jesus went to Galilee to call more disciples to join him. Seeing a man named Philip, Jesus said, "Follow me."

Philip then found his friend Nathanael and said to him, "We have found the person Moses and all the Scriptures promised!"

But Nathanael was not quite sure about Philip's news. After all, Jesus was from Nazareth - a small, poor, and unimportant town. How could the Savior of the world come from such a place?

Jesus saw Nathanael as he walked with Philip and said, "Nathaneal, come here!"

"Do we know each other?" Nathanael replied, knowing the two of them had never met.

Jesus did know him. He knew him well. Jesus said, "Before Philip called you, you were under a fig tree. I saw you."

How could Jesus have known this? Nathanael was stunned. "Rabbi, you are the Son of God! You are the King of Israel!" he proclaimed.

Jesus loved Nathanael's simple trust. Jesus looked at Nathanasl, saying, "You will see greater things than this. Heaven will open, and God's angels will come down to the Son of Man and then back up to God."

Of course, Jesus was talking about the story of Jacob and his ladder from Genesis. Jesus is the only way to come to God. A ladder will never get you any closer! God has to come to us. Now, in his Son Jesus, he had!

Ever since the Garden of Eden, when Adam and Eve turned their backs on their Creator, we have been apart from God. Some people try to earn God's love by doing lots of good things. But we can never do enough good to make God love us! Some people try to ignore God. But, just like Nathanael, he sees everyone! Others are just plain confused about what to make of God. Jesus loves people like that too! The book of John is for you and me and all types of people who need to know that Jesus is God.

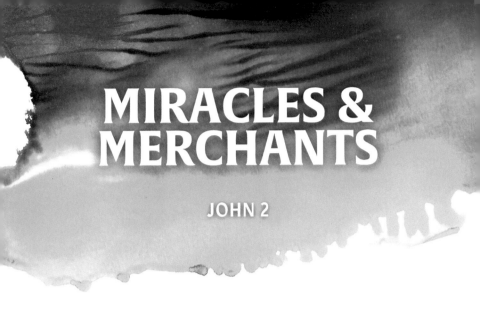

MIRACLES & MERCHANTS

JOHN 2

Two days after meeting Nathanael, Jesus traveled to a wedding in a town called Cana. As soon as Jesus arrived, it was clear that something was wrong.

Mary, Jesus's mother, anxiously ran to him and asked, "Son, can you do anything? We have run out of wine for the party!"

Now, you should know that while many of us are too young to drink wine today, it was very common for people of all ages back in Jesus's time.

You should also know that there was more going on here than meets the eye. This story is about something far greater than just having a drink. You see, the Old Testament spoke about wine as a sign of joy. It was a way of talking about God being with his people.

During the hundreds of years Israel waited for Jesus to come, they had grown spiritually thirsty. Jesus wanted his friends to see that, while they were dry now, a life-giving, soul-quenching, heart-softening time had come!

Jesus found several stone jars and asked the servants to fill each one to the top with water. Altogether, it was about 150 gallons. More than two bathtubs filled to the brim!

The master of the feast drew the first cup from the jars as the crowd looked on with nervous anticipation. Could the water have somehow turned to wine?

With great surprise, the master proclaimed, "This is some of the best wine I have ever tasted!"

It was a miracle! Who could do something so marvelous except the Son of God? The kingdom of Jesus was coming. It would refresh, renew, and redeem everything it touched.

The disciples were elated. With joy in their hearts, they traveled with Jesus to Jerusalem for Passover - a celebration the Jews held every year to remember how God saved them from slavery in Egypt many, many years before.

Jewish men and women came from all over to Jerusalem for Passover. Every year, people brought animals to sacrifice as a part of the festivities. Often, people would travel from far-off distances, making this quite a chore!

Some merchants in Jerusalem decided to take advantage of this problem by selling animals. They set up shop selling oxen, sheep, and pigeons right outside the temple. The holiest of days was becoming little more than a way for people to make money!

Jesus commanded, "Take these things away from my Father's house! Destroy this temple, and I will raise it back up in three days." He drove the merchants away with a whip and flipped over their tables.

Jesus's anger was unlike anything the disciples had seen before. He was angry, make no mistake! But, he was like a father who saves his child from danger by any means necessary. Jesus loved his children and wanted to win their hearts back from evil.

Bewildered, the Jews replied, "Jesus, don't be silly, it took us 46 years to build the temple. Now you want us to destroy it? What are you talking about?"

Jesus, though, was not talking about the building. He was referring to his own body. Not very long after that day, Jesus would die for the sins of the whole world, including the merchants whose tables he'd just overturned. Most people thought Jesus's death would destroy him. But only three days later, he would be raised from the dead.

As his disciples thought about their day at the temple, they began to understand, all the more, that their teacher was someone special. And of course, he was.

The one God had promised all along was here.

NEW LIFE

JOHN 3

As word spread about Jesus, the Pharisees grew more and more disgusted. But Nicodemus, a Pharisee, saw something different. Nicodemus just had to meet Jesus! Secretly, under cover of night so nobody would see him, Nicodemus went to see Jesus.

"Rabbi," Nicodemus whispered so only Jesus could hear, "I know you are a teacher from God. Nobody else could do the amazing signs and wonders you have done unless God is with him."

Jesus replied, "My signs and wonders point to an even greater miracle."

"What is it?" Nicodemus asked.

Jesus answered, "The kingdom of God is coming. But you will not see it unless you become new. It must be as if you were born all over again." Perplexed, Nicodemus asked, "How can you go back into your mother and be born again?"

"No, no," Jesus explained. "You must be born again of the Spirit. Your body will look the same, but your heart will be brand new. You will have a new reason for living. Only then can you see the kingdom of God."

Jesus looked more intently at Nicodemus, speaking some of the most beautiful words in the Bible. "God loved the world so much that He gave his one and only Son. Whoever believes this will not spiritually die but will have eternal life. God did not send me to point out how wrong everyone is, but rather to save God's friends. Because all people are sons of Adam and daughters of Eve, everyone already deserves death for their sins. I came to shine light into the darkness, show you your wickedness, and point you to the life you can have in God."

After his time with Nicodemus, Jesus and his disciples went to the Judean countryside. The water there was plentiful, making it a delightful place for Jesus to baptize new believers. Not too far from where Jesus was, another man named John was baptizing people. Remember him? Some of John's disciples approached him, saying, "The man you told us about is here baptizing. Look, everyone is going to Jesus instead of you. Aren't you jealous?"

John replied, "I am not the Christ, but I came to tell you that he was coming. My joy is complete because he is now here. He must increase, and I must decrease. He wants to tell us about God and give us the Holy Spirit. God has given all things to Jesus, and he is here to give those things to us."

Have you ever looked forward to a big birthday present that you wanted for a long, long, long time? You may have even waited for so long that you thought you would never get it. But then, you did!

That must have been what John's disciples felt at this very moment. Their moms and dads, grandparents, great-grandparents, and even their great-great-great-grandparents waited for Jesus to come. Now, he was here!

John finished talking to his followers with encouragement and a warning. "Whoever believes in Jesus will have eternal life. Though your body will die one day, your soul will be with God in heaven. But those who do not believe will have a life of eternal punishment, for they will get what their sins deserve."

A SAMARITAN WOMAN

JOHN 4

The Pharisees soon heard about all that Jesus was doing, and, once again, they were not happy!

Remember, Pharisees believed they could earn God's love by following every law in the Bible. But that is quite a silly idea because sin makes living a perfect life impossible.

Jesus heard about the Pharisees' anger and fled Judea for Galilee, sensing he was in danger. Most everyone would take a long, inconvenient route around a place called Samaria when making this trip. People did everything they could to stay out of Samaria! Why was this so?

You see, the Samaritans were part Jewish (people who could trace their family's history back to Abraham) and part Gentile (those who were not related to Abraham). Jews and non-Jews alike despised Samaritans. How sad and lonely it must have been to be from Samaria!

But Jesus loved the Samaritans. They were people just like you and me! Samaritans were made in God's image just as much as anyone else.

When Jesus arrived in Samaria, it was noon. The weather was quite warm, so Jesus sat down to rest near a well.

Just then, a woman came to draw water from the well. Gathering water at this time of day was rather unusual. Women generally gathered water only in the morning or evening. If someone was at the well at this time of day, they usually had done something wrong and could not be seen out and about.

Looking at the woman, Jesus asked, "Would you mind if I had a drink?"

Stunned, the woman replied, "How is it that you, a Jewish man, ask me, a woman from Samaria, for a drink?"

Jesus answered her with compassion, "If you knew God's gift, you would have asked me for a drink, and I would have given you living water."

Confused, the woman asked, "Sir, you have nothing to draw the water with, and the well is deep. Where do you get this living water?"

Jesus replied, pointing to the well, "Everyone who drinks this water will be thirsty again, but whoever drinks the water that I give will never thirst. My water is like a spring inside each person, welling up to eternal life."

The woman replied, "Can I have some of this water?"

Knowingly, Jesus told her, "Go, call your husband, and both of you come to me."

"But I have no husband," the woman responded.

Jesus knew this woman, even though they had never met in person. He knew her heart and what she had done. Jesus knew her better than she knew herself, and so he said, "I know that you do not have a husband. Instead, you have treated five men like they are your husband. You might think it's impossible for God to love someone like you. But living water is not for people who think they follow all the rules. It is for those who know they can't and need a Savior."

The woman replied, "I know the Messiah is coming. He will be called the Christ. When he comes, he will tell us all things."

Jesus looked at her intently, saying, "I am the one you have waited for."

The woman immediately ran through the town telling everyone, "Come, see a man who told me everything I ever did. Can this be the Christ?"

Meanwhile, the disciples urged Jesus to eat something. But Jesus said to them, "I have food to eat that you do not know about yet. What fills me is the love of my Father. Look and see; the fields are ripe for harvest. People are ready to receive the good news of the gospel. Those who have gone before us sowed the seeds of faith. The seeds have grown in people like this woman. Many hoped this day would come. Now, your job is to gather people to drink the living water and to tell them the good news of the gospel."

Many Samaritans believed in Jesus that day.

Jesus's mission was becoming clearer by the day. He did not come to save those who think they are good. His love is for those who think they don't deserve it; those who know they are not good enough. To those who know they have nothing, Jesus gives everything!

A POOLSIDE HEALING

JOHN 5

After his time with the Samaritans, Jesus continued his travels. One day, he came to a pool of water called Bethesda in the town of Jerusalem. Men and women with illnesses, diseases, and injuries gathered there every day, believing the water held the power to heal.

One man, in particular, had been unable to walk for 38 years. Jesus saw him lying on a mat beside the pool and asked, "Do you want to be healed?"

Did he ever!

"Sir, I cannot lift myself into the pool. Can you help?" he asked, not knowing who he was talking to.

Of course, this man did not need a pool of miracle water. He needed Jesus, the living water.

Jesus simply said, "Get up, pick up your mat, and walk." At once, the man was healed and rose to his feet. He skipped around like nothing was ever wrong! Can you imagine the air brushing against your cheeks as you run around for the first time?

You would think the whole town would break out in celebration. Typically, you'd be right. But there was a problem. It was the Sabbath.

God said that we are to honor the Sabbath and treat it as a special day. It helps us remember that God rested after six days of work when he created the world. Today, you might notice that many people do this on Sundays.

But over time, the Jews made up hundreds of silly rules about what you could and could not do on the Sabbath. It made them feel good about themselves when they obeyed these rules. It also gave the Jews a way to make others feel guilty when they didn't.

The Jews spoke harshly with the healed man, "It is the Sabbath. You know what the rules say! You cannot carry anything today, not even something so small as your mat."

How disheartening this must have been! After 38 years, this man could walk for the first time. But the Jews were more concerned about him breaking one of their pretend rules!

The man replied, "Jesus, God's Son, healed me. He told me to pick up my mat."

As you can imagine, the Jews were not happy! To heal this man, Jesus had "worked" on the Sabbath. Now, he had the nerve to claim God as his own Father.

Jesus heard the commotion and spoke to the Jews, saying, "My Father is working, and so am I. You have made up rules about the Sabbath to make yourselves feel more holy than you are. But these rules will not get you any closer to God.

"This man's healing is just the beginning of what I have the power to do. I will do greater works than these, and you will be amazed. Whoever believes in me has eternal life. Those who believe I am the Son of God may die here on earth, but their souls will live forever with my Father in heaven. I know this is true because the Father made me the judge. If you believe in me, you will not come under judgment, but will have life."

Jesus continued, "You listened to John the Baptist, but you would not believe him when he spoke of me. You honor Moses, but you cannot see that I am greater than him. You study the Scriptures because you think that just by knowing them, you will somehow gain eternal life. But the Scriptures themselves tell you that you cannot have eternal life without me."

Jesus's words should have moved the Jews deeply in their minds and hearts. After all, Moses and John the Baptist were two highly regarded people!

The light of the world was here. The living water was flowing right in front of the Jews. But their eyes were like those of a blind man and their ears like one who is deaf.

As you will see throughout the book of John, the Jews and Jesus disagreed about almost everything. The very one the Scriptures hoped for was standing right before them, ready to give them eternal life. Yet they could not receive the gift.

This unbelief led the Jews down a very twisted, evil path.

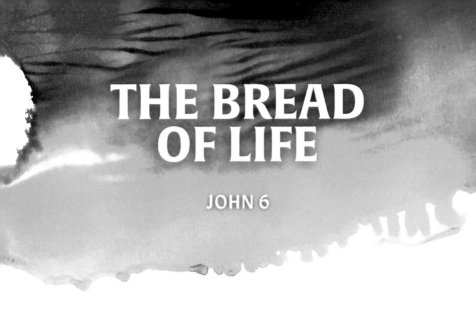

THE BREAD OF LIFE

JOHN 6

Jesus eventually made his way to a place called the Sea of Tiberias. Seeing that Jesus was no ordinary person, quite a large group began following him. Just as the crowd's size swelled to over 5,000 people, a number no one had seen to this point, the time had come for Passover.

You may remember from earlier in this book that Passover was a feast the Jews celebrated each year to remember how God saved the Israelites when their great-great-great-grandparents were slaves in Egypt.

Jesus looked at Philip, asking, "Where will we buy enough bread for all these people to eat?"

Of course, Jesus had a plan, but he wanted to test Philip. Philip thought for a moment while looking out at the crowd and replied, "I don't think even 200 denarii (over six months' wages!) worth of bread would be enough."

One of the disciples, Andrew, suggested, "There is a boy here who has five barley loaves and two fish, but that is not nearly enough!"

What would Jesus do? There was no way he could feed all these people. Right?!

"Everyone take a seat," Jesus requested as he took the loaves from the boy. He gave thanks to his Father and then began to pass the bread to all who were seated. Jesus did the same with the fish. Everyone ate as much as they wanted.

Once everyone was full, the disciples gathered all the uneaten food. There was more food leftover than when they started. Twelve baskets of bread!

When the people saw this, they were amazed, saying, "We waited for so long to meet Jesus! Now, he has come to save the world."

But Jesus, knowing the Jews were hiding right around the corner, journeyed to the mountain beside the sea and hid by himself.

That evening, the disciples got into a boat to travel across the sea to Capernaum. But Jesus was nowhere to be found.

A strong wind began to howl. A storm rolled in, and the ship was tossed to and fro. Jesus, however, was still missing!

After drifting nearly four miles, out of the corner of their eyes, the disciples saw Jesus.

Could it really be him!? Jesus was walking on water!

Jesus said to the disciples, "Do not be afraid; it is me."

How amazed the disciples must have been as they saw Jesus walking toward them on top of a stormy sea. How glad the disciples were as Jesus climbed into the boat! Very quickly, they arrived in Capernaum.

The next day the crowds piled into their boats and set sail to follow Jesus and the disciples. Jesus looked at the people and said, "You follow me because I gave you bread to eat. But do not work for the bread that leaves you hungry. Instead, work for the bread that gives you eternal life."

Jesus knew that no matter how much bread he gave the people, they would always need more. The bread he gave was supposed to show them that they needed something more, something better.

Jesus continued, "To get the bread of life, you must believe that I was sent from heaven by my Father, God. Remember Moses? God gave him bread from heaven. God's people rejoiced. But they were hungry again in the morning.

"But now, God has sent something far greater...me! I am the bread of life. If anyone eats this bread, they will never hunger or thirst. They will live forever!"

The Jewish leaders heard every word Jesus spoke and were not pleased! They grumbled amongst themselves, "Who is this man who claims to be from heaven? Isn't he the son of Joseph and Mary?"

The disciples heard Jesus' words too, and were perplexed, saying, "Jesus talks about things in a way we have never heard before! How can we believe him?"

Jesus replied, "It is hard to believe something so wonderful! That is why the Spirit has to help you understand. No one will trust in me unless my Father first gives them the Spirit. But some of you will not believe."

Jesus knew their hearts. He knew one of his disciples did not and would not believe. His name was Judas.

Judas, one of the twelve, was Jesus's enemy. His unbelief would lead him down a very twisted and wicked path.

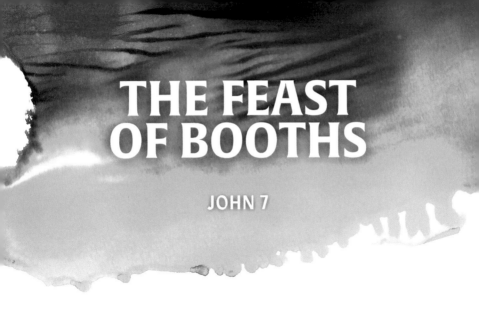

THE FEAST OF BOOTHS

JOHN 7

For Jesus, life grew more and more dangerous by the day. He was free to go about in Galilee, but the moment he stepped foot in the region of Judea, he knew what would happen. The Jews wanted him dead, but Jesus knew his time to die had not yet come.

It was October, which meant the Jews were celebrating the Feast of Booths. During this time, to remember God's kindness to their great-great-great-grandparents when they were in the wilderness after escaping from Egypt, the Jews camped out in tents made of leaves and sticks.

Jesus's disciples suggested he go down to Judea for the celebration to show people the works he was doing.

"No way!" Jesus replied. "It is not time for people to know who I am. You disciples go to the feast and leave me behind."

But as the disciples made their way to Galilee, Jesus sneaked down to Judea himself and hid amongst the crowds at the feast.

During the middle of the feast, Jesus went up to the temple and began teaching. The Jews marveled at what they heard.

"My teaching is not mine," Jesus proclaimed. "It is my Father's. I do not seek my fame and glory, but my Father's."

But the crowds did not see eye to eye with Jesus and began shouting, "This man must have a demon inside him!"

A group of men from Jerusalem questioned, "If we think he has a demon, why don't we just kill him?"

But nobody would kill Jesus on this day. It was not a part of God's plan. Many people still needed to hear God's good news. That day many people believed in Jesus at the feast.

Jesus continued to speak to those gathered, "I will be with you a little while longer, and then I must go to be with my Father. Where I am going, you cannot come."

These words, of course, confused the crowds. Where was Jesus going?

On the last day of the feast, Jesus cried out in a loud voice, "If anyone is thirsty, come to me and drink. As the Scripture says, whoever believes in me, 'Out of his heart will flow rivers of living water.'"

Jesus, of course, was speaking about the Holy Spirit. A few years after this feast, Jesus would die and go to be with his Father. The Spirit would come to his people to give them the love they always craved and reassure them that they are God's children. This "water" would never leave them wanting and would never leave them thirsty.

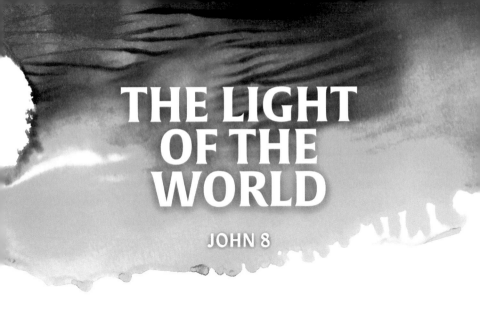

THE LIGHT OF THE WORLD

JOHN 8

One morning, Jesus was at the temple when the scribes and Pharisees brought a woman to him.

"This woman is married," they explained. "But she was pretending to be another man's wife. The law of Moses says we should throw stones at her as punishment. What do you think we should do?"

The big, important men were trying to test Jesus. If he did not obey the law of Moses, which said this woman must be stoned, they would have a charge to bring against him.

What would Jesus do?

Jesus bent down. But it was not to pick up a stone. Instead, he started writing on the ground.

Jesus then stood and asked, "Are any of you without sin? If you are, please, throw the first stone at this woman."

The men had never seen such love and wisdom together in one person. As the big, important men fled, Jesus looked at the woman and offered comfort. "Where did the men go? They are sinners, just like you. I do not condemn you. I have come to give you life. Go and sin no more."

But the Pharisees were not done questioning Jesus. His love for the world was far beyond their ability to understand. So, Jesus tried to use a word picture to help.

Jesus explained, "I am the light of the world. Whoever follows me will not walk in darkness but will have the light of life."

The Pharisees angrily replied, "You cannot claim these things! God did not send you."

"Believe what you want," Jesus answered. "I know where I came from and where I'm going. You only see what you can see with your eyes, and you cast some pretty harsh judgments on people! I can see people's hearts, and I judge no one. I came to give life. But you will die in your sins unless you believe that my Father sent me."

Still, the Pharisees could not understand.

Jesus continued, "Just as Moses lifted the serpent in the wilderness, so you will lift me up. You will try to kill me, but it will only bring me to my Father in heaven. Even now, my Father is with me. He has not left me, and I always do the things that bring him joy."

As Jesus was speaking, many in the crowd believed in him. Jesus turned to those who believed and said, "You are no longer slaves to sin. You have been set free."

But the new Jewish believers were not so sure. "How do we know you are not just a regular person with a demon living inside you?"

Jesus replied, "I do not have a demon, but I honor my Father. I do not seek my own fame. I want my Father to get all the glory. Those who believe in my words will never see death. Instead, they will go to be with my Father in heaven."

But the Jews could not understand. "Are you greater than Abraham? He died, and all the other prophets died too. How are you any different?"

"Abraham longed to see the day I would come. He believed God would send a rescuer to save the world from death. Abraham knew me, and he was glad. Now, I have come to you!" Jesus explained.

Confused, the Jews said, "But you are not yet 50 years old; how is it that you have been with Abraham?"

"Truly, truly, I say to you, before Abraham was, I am. I was with my Father in heaven from before the creation of the world," Jesus explained.

The Jews had enough! They picked up stones to throw at him, but Jesus quickly left and hid.

It can be hard to believe in someone as marvelous as Jesus because it means we have to admit there is something wrong with us; that we are sinners in need of rescue.

It is hard to admit that maybe we haven't had life "all figured out" and perhaps we have even been very wrong. But Jesus knows all of that. He sees everything, and yet he still chooses to forgive us and love us.

A MAN BORN BLIND

JOHN 9

Imagine for a moment that you have never seen anything. Nothing. Not a sunrise or a mountain or even what your parents look like. There was a man like this who met Jesus. His life would never be the same.

"This man," the disciples announced to Jesus, "was born blind. Who sinned that caused him to be born blind? This man? His parents?"

It was common in those days to think of conditions like blindness as God's punishment for sin. But Jesus could see what the disciples couldn't. He had a beautiful plan in mind for this man.

"This man is blind so you would see God's works through him," Jesus explained. "I am the light of the world. As long as I am in the world, I will bring light where you only see darkness."

Just then, Jesus knelt to the ground and did the strangest thing. He spit in the dirt to make mud. Then, Jesus took the mud and smeared it on the man's eyes. Just as God made life from the dust of the ground at the beginning of the Bible, so Jesus brought life to these broken eyes.

"Go, wash your eyes," Jesus said.

Immediately, the man could see for the first time in his life! His neighbors and those in the city were shocked. "How can you now see?" the people asked, halfway disbelieving it was even the same man.

The man told the townspeople about the mud and that it was Jesus who healed him. Upon hearing this, the people called in the Pharisees.

As delightful as this miracle was - a blind man could now see! - the Pharisees were still blind in their own way. They could not see past their make-believe rules they loved so much. This healing, after all, had taken place on the Sabbath!

The Pharisees questioned Jesus, "How is it that you claim to be from God, and yet you do not keep the Sabbath?" Looking at the formerly blind man, they asked, "Who do you say this man, Jesus, is?"

The man answered, "He is a prophet. I do not know anything else about him. But I do know that I was blind and now I can see. It's an amazing thing! Never since the world began has anyone heard of someone opening the eyes of a man like me who was born blind. If Jesus were not from God, he could not have done this."

Outraged, the Pharisees sent him away. But Jesus, seeing the man, brought him near.

Looking at the man in love, Jesus said, "I am the Son of Man, the one the Jews hoped would come to rescue the world. You have seen me. Do you believe?"

"Lord, I believe," the man replied as he fell down and worshipped Jesus.

Jesus came to renew the weary, to fix what is broken, and to heal those who are sick. Those who were humble enough to receive Jesus as a healer when they met him were given eyes to see God's kingdom. But those who thought they didn't need Jesus chose not to see that they were also weary or broken or sick.

Some of the Pharisees nearby asked, "Are we blind?"

Jesus said to them, "If you were blind, you would have no guilt. But now that you have seen my works, you are guilty of not believing in God's Son."

THE GOOD SHEPHERD

JOHN 10

Have you ever experienced something so beautiful that words alone failed to capture its splendor? Jesus is like that. His glory is unlike anything the world has ever known. He is the light of the world. But just one word picture is not enough to describe all the beauty of God's only Son.

Speaking to the Pharisees, Jesus explained, "The shepherd's sheep come in and out through the door. The sheep hear the shepherd's voice, and he calls them his own. But some people try to trick the shepherd's heard by climbing in another way. But the sheep know when there is an imposter in their midst, and they will not follow them. They only follow the shepherd's voice."

The Pharisees could not understand the wisdom of Jesus's words.

Jesus continued, "I am the door of the sheep. Anyone who comes through the door that I open will come into my pasture and find rest."

The Pharisees began to understand that Jesus was speaking against them. The Pharisees were the imposter shepherds because they believed they could follow enough rules to make God love them. But Jesus wanted them to see that just as a sheep cannot open a door on their own and can do nothing to impress the shepherd, so it is with those who enter God's kingdom. It is a gift that God must give, not because of how good we have been or how many rules we have followed. He lets sheep in simply because he loves them.

Jesus kept speaking, "If someone is hired to care for a flock of sheep and a wolf comes, the hired person will run and flee. He will leave the sheep to be killed by the wolf because he does not truly care for the sheep. But I am the good shepherd. I know my own, and my own know me, just as the Father knows me, and I know the Father. Because of my love for the sheep, I lay down my life for them. I have lots of other sheep out wandering the countryside. I must find them and bring them in too."

The Jews began to fight with each other over these words. Some said Jesus had a demon inside him. Others said that someone who could heal a blind man couldn't possibly be controlled by a demon.

Months later, at a feast in Jerusalem, the Jews again questioned Jesus, saying, "How long will you keep us in suspense? If you are the Christ, stop using these silly word pictures and tell us you are."

Jesus replied, "I did tell you, but you did not believe. The works I do, my healings and miracles, tell you who I am. But you do not believe because you are not my sheep. My sheep hear my voice, I know them, and they follow me. I give them eternal life, they will never experience death, and no one will take them from me. My Father, who is greater than all, has given them to me. The Father and I are one."

The Jews boiled with anger! How could this man claim to be one with God? They gathered stones and readied themselves to hurt, and maybe kill, Jesus.

But Jesus answered them calmly, "You cannot stone me, for I have done nothing wrong. I have shown you many good works from my Father. For which of them will you stone me?"

Seeing his wisdom, the Jews tried to arrest him instead. But Jesus escaped from their hands and went across the Jordan River to where John had been baptizing earlier. Many came to Jesus there beside the Jordan and believed, agreeing, "Everything John said about this man is true."

LAZARUS

JOHN 11

Days later, Jesus's friends, Mary and Martha, hurried to tell him the bad news. Their brother and Jesus's dear friend, Lazarus, was sick.

Upon hearing the news, though, Jesus declared, "This illness will not lead to death. His illness is for God's glory, so that the Son of God may also receive glory."

Two days later, Jesus traveled to Bethany, the town where Lazarus lived with his sisters. Jesus said to his disciples, "Our friend Lazarus has fallen asleep, but I will go to wake him up."

Confused, the disciples replied, "Lord, if he is asleep, he will wake up on his own."

Jesus answered plainly, "Lazarus has died."

Wait! Didn't Jesus say this illness would not lead to death? He did, but very soon Jesus would teach his friends a valuable lesson about life with him.

When the disciples and Jesus arrived in Bethany, Lazarus had already been dead for four days. Many Jews had traveled the two miles from Jerusalem to comfort Mary and Martha during this sad time.

Martha went to Jesus, claiming, "If you had been here, my brother would not have died."

Jesus answered her with love. "Your brother will rise again. I am the resurrection and the life. Whoever believes in me, though his body dies, will live with me forever. Do you believe this?"

"Yes, Lord. I believe that you are the Christ, the Son of God," Martha replied, trusting what she could not yet see.

Martha called Mary to come quickly. As soon as she saw him, Mary fell at Jesus's feet, saying, "If you had been here, my brother would not have died."

Jesus saw her weeping. He looked around and saw the other Jews gathered in Bethany crying as well. His heart broke with love, and his spirit was troubled because of the people's sadness.

Jesus cried as he asked, "Where is Lazarus?"

The women took Jesus to the tomb. It was a cave with a stone in front of it. The stone was rolled away in an eerie preview of what was to happen in Jesus's own life.

Jesus lifted his eyes to heaven and said, "Father, I thank you that you have heard me."

Then, in a loud voice, Jesus cried, "Lazarus, come out!" At once, Lazarus stood up and walked out of the cave.

Jesus wanted us to see that, in him, there is no fear of death. Those who believe in Jesus will see their physical bodies die on earth. But their souls will live forever in heaven.

Astounded by what they had seen, many Jews believed in Jesus that day. But some went to the Pharisees to tell them what Jesus had done.

These Pharisees gathered with the chief priest, Caiaphas. Together, they agreed that the only way to stop Jesus was to kill him.

From that day forward, they made plans to put an end to Jesus's life.

OINTMENT & BRANCHES

JOHN 12

How do you say "thank you" to someone who raised your brother from the dead? You could have a big parade or write a really nice thank-you note. But Mary, Lazarus's sister, had something else in mind.

She removed her most expensive ointment from the shelf, bent down, and rubbed it on Jesus's feet. The house filled with its sweet fragrance as she wiped his feet with her hair.

This scene may seem strange to us today, but in Jesus's time this was an extravagant show of love. Mary loved Jesus with her whole heart.

Rubbing ointment on people's feet was not only a dirty, stinky job, but was usually the work of servants. Also, women rarely took their hair down in public. Mary loved Jesus a lot!

But Judas, one of the disciples, was lurking nearby. He would soon betray Jesus and said, "What a waste! Why didn't you sell the ointment and give the money to help the poor?"

Jesus answered, "Leave her alone so that she can keep the ointment for my burial day. You will always have the poor with you, but you will not always have me."

When the crowds heard Jesus was in town, they came to see that Lazarus was, in fact, alive. The chief priests, seeing Lazarus, made plans to kill him as well as Jesus.

The next day, those same crowds heard that Jesus was coming to Jerusalem. People collected palm branches, waved them in the air, and ran out to meet him, crying out, "Hosanna! Blessed is he who comes in the name of the Lord, the King of Israel!"

The palm branches were a sign of victory. People thought Jesus would come to rescue them from their enemies. In a way, they were right.

You see, Jesus's followers were under the harsh rule of the Roman government. Would Jesus come to rescue them from Rome?

What the new believers couldn't see is they had a much bigger enemy - sin. Rome could make their lives difficult on earth, but sin would make their lives miserable for eternity. They were hoping for a mighty warrior to save them from Rome, but what they really needed was a Savior to rescue them from sin.

As the people waved their branches, Jesus rode into Jerusalem on a young, baby donkey. You see, he didn't need to prove his power with a thoroughbred horse, and he didn't need to show his strength with a big, fancy chariot. His power and strength came from the one who carved the mountains and filled the oceans with water. His gentleness came from the one who spoke baby donkeys into existence. Jesus wasn't the type of king that people expected. But he was, and is, the type of king our hearts truly need.

The crowds following Jesus grew larger and larger. People heard about Jesus raising Lazarus from the dead. Many believed in him and told others about how he came to raise us both to life on earth and then forever to eternal life.

But to give eternal life, Jesus had to come to Jerusalem to do one thing. He had to die. He had to take the punishment we deserve for our sins.

Speaking to his disciples, Jesus said, "Unless a grain of wheat falls to the ground and dies, it remains alone. But, if it dies, it bears much fruit. Whoever loves his life on earth more than what is to come in heaven will only see life on earth. But whoever sees eternal life as more valuable than life on earth will live forever. Those who follow me will be with me in heaven with my Father. My soul is troubled that I must die, but this is the reason I came into the world. Father, glorify your name. Show the world that you are wonderful and worthy of praise!"

Just then, a voice boomed from heaven, "I have glorified it, and I will glorify it again."

The crowd looked at one another in shock. Some heard the voice while others claimed it was just thunder.

Jesus assured them, "The voice came for your sake, not mine. Now is the time when the ruler of this world, Satan, will be cast out. And I, when my Father lifts me up, will bring all my people to me. I am the light of the world. I will be with you a little while longer, and then I will be gone. Follow the light so that you may become children of the light and tell the world about me."

After Jesus said these things, he departed and hid. Though he had done many signs to show who he was, the Pharisees still would not believe. But their unbelief was not because Jesus wasn't persuasive. It was to fulfill what the prophet Isaiah said, "He has blinded their eyes and hardened their hearts." Rather than hindering God's plan, this was further proof that Jesus is God's Son.

THE BETRAYER

JOHN 13

Jesus's love was bigger, deeper, wider, and taller than any the world had ever known. He loved the world his Father made, and he loved people perfectly. He didn't just say, "I love you," when it was easy. Jesus was a servant who would love his people through indescribable pain and suffering, all the way to his death.

Love like this doesn't just come out of the clear blue sky. Jesus could love because his Father had loved him in inexpressible ways. He was sure of what he had come to the world to do. Jesus knew the Father had given all things to him and that he was going back to heaven after his time on Earth.

One night at supper, Jesus did the unthinkable to show his love for the disciples.

One by one, Jesus washed his disciples' feet.

Simon Peter, one of the disciples, did not understand and protested, "Never! You will never wash my feet. That is a job for servants, and you are the Lord."

Jesus answered, "Simon, I know this is quite unusual, but it is what you need. Unless I wash you, you cannot be with me."

Of course, Jesus was not just talking about Simon Peter's feet. Even more than having his feet washed, Simon Peter needed his heart cleansed as well.

Looking around at the disciples, Jesus said, "Not all of you are clean. One of you will betray me."

The disciples looked at one another in shock, wondering who it was. Jesus, of course, knew about Judas. But none of the disciples knew there was a bad apple in their bunch until now.

When Jesus finished washing the disciples' feet, he leaned in and asked them, "Do you understand what I have done for you? Now, you must wash one another's feet. You must follow my example of love for others."

After saying these things, Jesus grew deeply troubled. The coming betrayal weighed heavily on his heart.

The disciples demanded, "Who is it? Which of us will betray you?"

Jesus replied, "Whoever I give this morsel of bread to is the one who will betray me."

Jesus leaned forward and gave the bread to Judas. When Judas ate the morsel, Satan entered him. "Do what you are going to do quickly," Jesus asked.

At once, Judas sprang from the table and ran out into the night.

Jesus looked around at the remaining disciples and comforted them, saying, "Soon I will go to be with my Father. You cannot come with me but must stay behind a while. But you have seen and felt my love. Love one another in the same way. The whole world will know you are my followers when they see how you love one another."

Simon Peter was once again confused. "Where are you going?" he asked Jesus.

"Where I am going you cannot come," Jesus answered, "but you will follow afterward."

"But Jesus," Simon Peter replied, "why can't I go now? I will lay down my life for you."

Jesus simply said, "Do you think you are without sin? Would you lay down your life for me? I tell you, Simon Peter, you will deny me three times and then the rooster will crow."

MY FATHER'S HOUSE

JOHN 14

Jesus knew his disciples were most worried about where he was going, and when they would see him again. All of his words seemed wonderful. But, the disciples questioned, were they a little too fantastic to be true?

"Don't be troubled," Jesus comforted. "In my Father's house are many rooms. I will prepare a place for you so that you'll be with me forever."

Thomas asked, "Lord, we do not know where this house is. How will we know how to get there?"

"I am the way, the truth, and the life," Jesus answered. "No one comes to the Father except through me. You know me, and so you will also know the way to where I am going. If you know me, you also know the Father."

These words confused the disciples. The Father was in Jesus, and Jesus was in the Father. They loved one another so much that it was as if they were united together, yet still two separate persons.

As if having the Father and Jesus were not enough, Jesus had one more big promise!

"If you love me, you will keep my commandments. I will ask the Father, and he will give you another helper. He is the Spirit of truth, the Holy Spirit, and he will be with you forever. In fact, you already know him because he lives inside of you," Jesus assured them.

The Holy Spirit...living inside them? How was this possible? Why would God do that?

Jesus answered, "The Holy Spirit will help you know that you are never alone. He will show you that you have a love that will hold you forever, no matter where you go, what you do, or how big you mess up! If anyone loves me, he will keep my word, and my Father will love him, and we will come to him and make our home with him."

What wonderful news! The God who made all the twinkling stars in the sky, who comforted his people in the wilderness, who brought his children back home after the exile...this God was making his home with his people.

Sin makes our hearts want to run away from God, but, in love, God still wants to be near to us. Love like this melts our hearts and turns us from rebels into relatives - sons and daughters of God.

But all of that made the fact that Jesus had to leave all the more painful!

Jesus comforted the disciples, saying, "Peace I leave with you. Let not your hearts be troubled or afraid. I am going away, and I will come back. If you love me, you will rejoice because I am going to the Father. I am telling you all of this so that you will believe, even more, that what I say is true when it happens."

VINES & FRIENDS

JOHN 15-16:4

Jesus's kingdom was unlike anything the disciples had experienced before. For this reason, Jesus already used several word pictures to help the disciples understand what words alone cannot express: the infinite depth, wonder, and goodness of his love. He is the living water, the light of the world, the good shepherd, the door of the sheep, and now - the true vine.

Jesus explained, "My Father takes care of the vine and prunes the branches that do not bear fruit. Everyone who abides in me will bear much fruit. In other words, those who remain close to me, who get their nourishment from me, will be a blessing to the world. If you follow me, you will be like a branch on my vine."

What a beautiful picture of our need! Jesus is the giver of all life. Without him, we would wither and, spiritually speaking, die. But, through him we have life and then can bless the world around us.

"If you abide in me, and my words abide in you, ask whatever you wish, and it will be done for you. My Father is glorified when he gives his children what they ask for."

Jesus wanted his disciples to know that following him was not a drudgery, but a joy. He is the best father the world has ever known. But he doesn't stop with just calling us children.

Jesus continued, "I speak these things so that the joy I have for you overflows into your hearts. I want your joy to be complete. I want you to feel, through and through, how deeply God loves you. These words are my commandment, that you will love one another as I have loved you. The greatest love the world has ever known is this: that someone lays down his life for his friends. You are my friends if you love one another. No longer do I call you servants."

Friends?! It's already plenty wonderful that we are sons and daughters of the King. But King Jesus also wants to be our friend. He loves you and wants to spend time with you.

But there is something hard about being friends with Jesus. To be his friend meant the disciples would be enemies with the world.

Jesus assured the disciples, "If the world hates you, know that it hated me first. I have called you out of the world's ways. I want you to know this because the rejection you feel in this life will seem small compared to the acceptance you will have in the life to come."

If you follow Jesus, you may have felt this hurt and loneliness before. Often, God's desires for our life are not the same as what the world wants for us. It can make us feel left out and we might even want to disobey God just so we won't feel lonely.

God sees this struggle. Through Jesus, he wants us to know that his love is enough to hold us today, tomorrow, and for the rest of eternity. We are his friends...forever.

THE HOLY SPIRIT

JOHN 16:5-17

Jesus had even more to share with his disciples as they sat together. This speech, which goes all the way back to John 13 when Jesus washed his disciples' feet, is known today as the Upper Room Discourse. Jesus had already hinted that the Holy Spirit would come. Now, he was ready to tell the disciples more.

"Soon, I will go to be with my Father and I will send you the Holy Spirit. Not only will he tell the world the dirty, broken truth about sin, but he will point people to how they can be made clean and whole through me. When the Spirit comes, he will guide you into all truth. He will not speak on his own authority. He will listen to the Father and me and glorify us with how he leads you," Jesus explained.

The disciples were discouraged and said to one another, "What does all this mean? Jesus says he will be with us a little while and then go someplace we cannot yet go. But then again, in a little while, we will see him? How do we make sense of this?"

The disciples were too nervous to ask Jesus their questions. But Jesus knew what they wanted to ask and offered this comfort: "Truly, truly, I say to you, you will weep and be sad. Your hearts will fill with sorrow, but your pain will turn into joy. The sting of losing me will burn. But it will be like a woman giving birth. Delivering the baby is incredibly painful. But, once the baby arrives, there is an inexpressible joy, and the pain is forgotten!"

Jesus's words were all beginning to make sense to the disciples. Jesus was leaving, and, as sad as that news was, it was not the end.

Jesus looked at them thoughtfully, saying, "In this world you will have trouble. But take heart; I have overcome the world."

When Jesus spoke these words, he lifted his eyes to heaven and prayed a most beautiful prayer to his Father. "The hour has come. Take me to you, and I will glorify you. I have told the world about you; that those who believe in you will receive eternal life. Those who belong to you have believed, and I continue to pray for those who will come to believe in you and receive eternal life. Father, please unite those who trust in us and make them strong. The world does not like us, and so it does not like them. Strengthen them to stand strong when they are attacked because of their love for us. And now, just as we were together at the creation of the world, bring me to yourself."

DENIAL

JOHN 18

When Jesus finished praying, he walked with his disciples across a babbling brook and into a garden. It could have been a beautiful moment of togetherness, but Judas still had it on his heart to betray Jesus.

Judas called together a band of Roman soldiers and some of the chief priests and Pharisees. They approached Jesus with lanterns, torches of flaming fire, and weapons that could have killed even the mightiest of men. But Jesus was not surprised. He knew all this would happen because it had been a part of God's plan all along.

Jesus asked, "Who are you looking for?"

The big, important men answered, "We are looking for Jesus of Nazareth."

Boldly, Jesus answered, "I am he."

When Jesus said this, the big, important men fell to the ground in surprise. Jesus asked again, "Who is it you are looking for?"

The men answered, "Jesus of Nazareth."

Jesus answered, "I am he. If you are looking for me, please let my disciples go free." Jesus was the good shepherd. The Bible said that he would "not lose one" of his sheep. Even in his final days, Jesus protected those he loved.

But Simon Peter was not so sure. He drew his sword from his side, struck the high priest's servant's head, and cut off his ear!

Jesus commanded, "Peter, put your sword away! I must suffer and do my Father's will."

Immediately, the big, important men bound Jesus with ropes and arrested him. First, they led him to Annas, the former high priest. Annas's son-in-law, Caiaphas, was the high priest at the time. Caiaphas was the one who told the Jews it would be good for one man to die for all of Jesus's followers. God has a way of working in the details!

Simon Peter and one other disciple followed Jesus. The other disciple, who goes unnamed in the Bible, went with Jesus into the high priest's courtyard. Simon Peter stood outside the door and waited.

After a few minutes, the other disciple was able to sneak Simon Peter in with the help of a servant girl who kept watch over the door. However, to enter, Simon Peter had to deny Jesus and told the girl he was not a disciple.

Since the weather had grown cold, the servants and officers made a charcoal fire to warm themselves. Simon Peter was also with them as Annas began questioning Jesus.

Jesus said to Annas, "I have never tried to hide who I am. I have told the world that I can rescue them from their sin. I said nothing in secret. Ask any of your men who have heard me. They know what I said."

When he spoke these words, one of the officers struck Jesus with his hand, saying, "That is no way to speak to the high priest!"

"Why did you strike me?" Jesus protested. "I have said nothing wrong."

Annas then bound Jesus with ropes and sent him to his son-in-law, Caiaphas.

But Simon Peter was still warming himself by the fire. So, the officers asked, "You are not one of his disciples, are you?" Again, like a coward, Simon Peter denied Jesus, saying, "I am not."

One of the high priest's servants, a relative of the man whose ear Simon Peter had cut off, asked, "Didn't I see you in the garden?"

Again, Simon Peter denied it, and at once a rooster crowed. Remember, in the upper room Jesus told Simon Peter he would deny him three times, and then the rooster would crow. Jesus knew what lay ahead of him, down to the smallest detail.

Next, the soldiers led Jesus from the house of Caiaphas to meet with Pilate, the governor. Pilate asked the officers, "What has this man done wrong?"

After the Jews explained, Pilate instructed, "Take him yourselves and judge him by your own Jewish law." Pilate did not want to take responsibility, or the blame, for killing the Son of God.

But the Jews answered, "No, we need to judge him under Roman law. Jewish law will not allow us to put him to death." All of this was becoming more and more corrupt by the moment! The Jews were accusing Jesus of religious law-breaking. However, under Roman law nobody could be put to death for breaking a law of th Jews.

But they could be killed for claiming to be the king!

So, Pilate entered his headquarters and called to Jesus, "Are you the King of the Jews?"

Jesus answered wisely, "My kingdom is not of this world. If my kingdom were of this world, my servants would fight for me against the Jews. But my kingdom is not fit for the world as it is now. It is fit for heaven."

Pilate was puzzled. "So you are a king?"

Jesus answered, "You are the one saying I am a king! My purpose in coming to the world is to tell people about the good news of my Father. To tell people the truth - that they can be rescued from their sins. Everyone who is of the truth listens to my voice."

Pilate asked, "What is the truth?"

After Pilate said this, he went back to the Jews and told them, "I find no guilt in him. But you have a custom that I should release one prisoner to you each year. Do you want me to release to you the King of the Jews?"

But the Jews cried out, "Not him, but Barabbas, the robber!"

The Jews were merciless and would do anything to force Pilate to kill Jesus!

CRUCIFY HIM!

JOHN 19

As Pilate let Barabbas go free, he turned and began to beat Jesus violently with clubs and whips. Pilate's soldiers mocked Jesus by twisting together a crown of thorns for his head while draping his body in a purple robe. As the soldiers struck Jesus, over and over again, they shouted, "Hail, King of the Jews!"

Why the harsh treatment? Wasn't Pilate trying to send Jesus back to the Jews? While we can't quite connect all the dots on this question, what we do know is that Pilate was furious! The pressure from the Jews had certainly gotten under his skin and Jesus had thrown his empire into quite the uproar.

After Pilate got his cheap shots in on Jesus, he wanted no blood on his hands. So, he led Jesus back outside to the Jews, saying, "I find no guilt in him."

When the chief priests and officers saw Jesus, they began chanting loudly, "Crucify him, crucify him!"

Pilate said to them, "If you want to crucify him, you must do it yourself. I find no guilt in him."

The Jews replied, "Our law says that because Jesus claims to be the Son of God, he must die."

When Pilate heard this, he grew terribly afraid. His fear mounted as he remembered his wife's dream from the night before. In the dream, God told her that Jesus was innocent. Pilate leaned over to Jesus and asked, "Where are you from?"

But Jesus would not answer.

Pilate insisted, "Why won't you speak to me? Don't you know I have the power to set you free or kill you?"

Jesus answered, "You would have no power over me unless God had given it to you first."

Pilate was trying to release Jesus, but the Jews, wanting Pilate to kill him right then, cried out, "If you free him, you are turning your back on Rome."

But Pilate would have none of this reasoning. He saw through the Jews' plan and released Jesus, once and for all, to the Jewish leaders to be killed.

Jesus, already bloodied and exhausted, was made to carry the very cross he would be hung on to a spot just outside the city walls called The Place of the Skull.

There, in the most terrible, disgusting act of murder in history, the Jews killed Jesus.

Soldiers drove nails through Jesus's hands and feet.

But it isn't the pain or the bleeding that kills you in crucifixion. No, it is something far worse.

As Jesus hung there, he lost the strength to hold his own body up. He collapsed upon himself, unable to breathe. It was like drowning, but with plenty of air all around that he just couldn't seem to draw into his lungs.

Treated as a criminal, he was hung between two others. As the prophet Isaiah said, "He would be counted alongside the evildoers."

Above Jesus's cross, an inscription, placed there by Pilate to mock him, read "Jesus of Nazareth, King of the Jews." The words were written in three different languages, so everyone for miles around could read it.

As Jesus hung on the cross, the soldiers stripped him of his clothing. They divided his garments to take home as trophies.

Beside the cross stood three women, one of whom was Jesus's own mother. In a most painful moment, Jesus looked down at his mom and said, "Woman, behold, your son!"

Jesus then looked at John, saying, "Behold, your mother!" From that moment forward, John took Mary to his home and cared for her as if she was his own mother.

Then, Jesus, knowing that his time had come, declared, "I am thirsty."

A jar full of sour wine stood beside the cross. So, the soldiers soaked a sponge with it and held it up to Jesus's mouth. The wine was just enough to moisten his throat so he could proclaim in a loud voice, "It is finished!"

Jesus then bowed his head and gave up his spirit.

It was customary to leave the bodies of criminals hanging on crosses for several days for all in the city to see. However, the Passover was near, and so the Jews asked Pilate if he would break the criminals' legs and take them away. If they were not dead already, breaking their legs certainly would assure they were!

So, the soldiers came and broke the legs of the men on either side of Jesus. But when they came to Jesus and saw that he was already dead, they did not break his legs. Instead, a soldier pierced his side with a spear.

At once, from Jesus's side, flowed blood and water...living water, some might say.

After these things, two of Jesus's followers, Joseph of Arimathea and Nicodemus (remember him?) wrapped Jesus's body in linen, laid him in a tomb in a garden, and rolled a large, heavy stone to cover the entry.

Jesus, the long-awaited Son of God, was dead.

Jesus came into our world. He lived the life the Bible says we should, spotless and without sin. If anyone deserved the love of God, it was Jesus!

But, on this day, Jesus got our punishment. Not only did he receive the death we deserve, but God turned his face away and allowed it to happen. Jesus lost the very presence of his Father on the cross so that God can look at us in the way Jesus deserved - with a love that will hold you forever, no matter where you go, what you do, or how big you mess up!

RESURRECTION

JOHN 20

Three days later, Mary Magdalene visited the tomb where Jesus lay. But as she approached, something was different. Mary Magdalene was in for a surprise!

The large, heavy stone, placed there just a few days ago, had moved. Jesus was nowhere to be found! Mary Magdalene was with Jesus when he died just a few days before. How could he now be gone?

Mary Magdalene ran as fast as she could to Simon Peter and John. In a panic, she shouted, "They have taken the Lord. We do not know where he is!"

Simon Peter and John rushed to the tomb and saw it with their own eyes. The linen cloths were there, but Jesus was not! It was all becoming clear to Simon Peter and John now.

Jesus had been raised from the dead to be with his Father. It was just as he said it would be all along.

But Mary Magdalene still did not understand where Jesus went. She stood weeping as two angels came to comfort her, saying, "Woman, why are you crying?"

Mary Magdalene answered, "Someone has taken my Lord, and I do not know where he is."

After saying this, Mary turned around. Standing right in front of her was Jesus, but she could not recognize him.

Jesus spoke tenderly to her, "Why are you weeping? Who are you looking for?"

Thinking the man was a gardener, she demanded, "If you have taken Jesus away, tell me where he is."

Jesus looked at his friend, simply saying, "Mary."

Mary Magdalene immediately knew the voice calling her by name. Overjoyed, she threw her arms around Jesus!

Jesus said to her, "Do not cling to me, for I have not yet gone to be with my Father in heaven. Now, go to my brothers and say to them, 'Jesus is getting ready to go to his Father.'"

Mary Magdalene ran and gathered the disciples, proclaiming, "I have seen the Lord!"

As evening approached, the disciples locked themselves indoors for fear the Jews would come looking for them. Through the locked doors, Jesus appeared, showing them his hands and side and saying, "Peace be with you. As the Father has sent me, I am sending you into the world to tell others the good news."

Jesus stepped back and breathed on them. But it was no ordinary breath. Jesus said, "Receive the Holy Spirit, the one I said would come to be your Helper."

Now Thomas, one of the disciples, was not in the room when Jesus came. When the others told him about Jesus, he said, "Unless I see and feel where the nails and spear went into his body, I will never believe."

Eight days later, the disciples gathered again in the locked room. This time, Thomas was with them. Again, Jesus came, saying, "Peace be with you."

Then, looking at Thomas, Jesus said, "Put your finger here and see my hands. Put out your hand and place it in my side. Do not disbelieve, but believe."

Thomas gingerly placed his finger where the spear pierced Jesus's side, proclaiming, "My Lord and my God!"

But Jesus cautioned, "You have believed because you have seen me. Blessed are those who have not yet seen me and have believed."

Now Jesus did many other signs in the disciples' presence, which are not written in the book of John. But what is written here is so that you would believe that Jesus is the Christ, the Son of God, and that by believing you may have life in his name.

BREAKFAST

JOHN 21

Simon Peter, Thomas, Nathanael, John, and James gathered together by the Sea of Tiberias.

"Let's go fishing!" Simon Peter suggested. Of course, all of these men were fishermen by trade before they were Jesus's disciples. But this time, they were out of luck!

After fishing all night, the disciples didn't catch even one little fish!

Just as the sun rose over the horizon, Jesus appeared on the shore. But the disciples did not recognize him.

"Did you catch anything?" Jesus asked.

"No!" the disciples answered, frustrated after a long night.

"Why don't you cast your net on the right side of your boat? You'll catch plenty of fish there," Jesus suggested.

The disciples looked at one another. "Who was this man, and why was he giving these experienced fishermen advice?" they wondered.

But the disciples decided to give it a try.

So, with a heave and a ho, they tossed the net overboard. Minutes later, there were so many fish! The disciples couldn't even lift the net on the boat!

John leaned over to Simon Peter, saying, "That man must be the Lord."

Simon Peter, unable to contain his excitement, jumped in the water and swam to shore. The rest of the disciples followed in the boat while dragging the net full of fish.

When they got to land, the disciples saw fish cooking over a charcoal fire and bread.

Jesus said to the men, "Bring some of the fish you just caught."

So, Simon Peter hauled the net ashore and counted 153 large fish. There were so many fish; the strong net nearly tore in two!

The disciples now knew this man must be Jesus as he asked, "Why don't you come and have breakfast with me?"

Together, they enjoyed bread and their fresh catch of fish. When they finished, Jesus said to Simon Peter, "Simon, son of John, do you love me more than these disciples do?"

Simon Peter replied, "Yes, Lord; you know that I love you." "Feed my lambs," Jesus instructed. Then a second time, Jesus asked, "Simon, son of John, do you love me?

Again, Simon Peter answered, "Yes, Lord; you know that I love you."

"Tend my sheep," Jesus said. Then a third time, Jesus asked, "Do you love me?"

Once again, Simon Peter said, "Lord, you know everything; you know that I love you."

Jesus answered, "Feed my sheep. Truly, truly, I say to you, when you were young, you used to dress and walk wherever you wanted. But, you will stretch out your hands when you are old, and another will dress you and carry you where you do not want to go."

Of course, Jesus was talking about his death on the cross when his arms were stretched out and he was carried to his tomb. He also may have been telling Simon Peter about how he would die one day as well.

Simon Peter turned and saw John following them. Simon Peter asked Jesus, "Lord, what about this man?"

"What does it matter to you if he follows me? You remain with me and follow me as well. It is my will that he follows me to the end as well," Jesus said of John. He did this to show that John had the authority to speak about Jesus so that we know everything he says is true.

Now, there are many other things Jesus did. If every single one of them were recorded, the world itself could not contain the books the stories would fill.